Railway Moods

THE
WEST SOMERSET
RAILWAY

DON BISHOP

HALSGROVE

First published in Great Britain in 2005

Title page: Home based Manor class No.7820 Dinmore Manor climbing hard past Bye Farm near Washford with an afternoon Bishops Lydeard to Minehead service. 31 March 1997.

British Library Cataloguing-in-Publication Data
A CIP record for this title is available from the British Library

ISBN 1 84114 445 2

HALSGROVE
Halsgrove House
Lower Moor Way
Tiverton, Devon EX16 6SS
Tel: 01884 243242
Fax: 01884 243325
email: sales@halsgrove.com
website: www.halsgrove.com

Printed and bound by D'Auria Industrie Grafiche Spa, Italy

INTRODUCTION

T he West Somerset Railway is Britain's longest private/preserved railway, running for 23 miles from its junction with the mainline network at Norton Fitzwarren near Taunton, through rolling Somerset countryside and over some steep gradients to Minehead on the Bristol Channel coast. It is arguably one of the most scenic lines in the UK, with its very varied landscape from the Quantock Hills between Bishops Lydeard and Williton to the coast at Watchet and Blue Anchor.

The line was constructed in two parts, the first section being from Norton Fitzwarren to Watchet, authorised in 1857 at an estimated cost of £120,000. The line was to be built to Brunel's broad gauge, and indeed Brunel himself was appointed engineer. However, by this time he was in poor health and died before completion of the line. Construction started in 1859 and after some financial difficulties which saw costs rise above £180,000 the line was completed for trains to commence running in March 1862. Subsequently another company, the Minehead Railway Co., was formed to build an extension of the line from Watchet to Minehead. This was completed in 1874 and the whole 25 mile route worked by the Bristol & Exeter Railway Co. until that company was taken over by the Great Western Railway in 1876. The line having been built to the broad gauge presented some restrictions in early days in respect of through working to other parts of the UK by goods traffic. The directors of the line persuaded the GWR to convert the line to the standard gauge, work being completed over one weekend in 1882, some ten years before the broad gauge's final demise.

Minehead grew in popularity as a seaside resort quite rapidly at the start of the twentieth century and improvements were carried out to the line by the GWR, who had taken over from the independent companies in 1922. These improvements involved extra loops to allow trains to cross and lengthening of platforms. By the 1950's 'holidays by rail' boom, the line was always busy, particularly on Summer Saturdays with through trains from the Midlands, North of England and London. The opening of the Butlin's holiday camp at Minehead in 1962 kept the line busy, but with the increasing use of the motor car as a means of transportation and the publication of the infamous Beeching report in 1963, the line was listed for closure. A campaign to prevent closure was initially successful, but doom and gloom prevailed as economies were made and the line fell into decay and a certain degree of dereliction. The much reduced service was finally withdrawn with effect from 2 January 1971.

Following this a campaign was launched to re-open the line under private ownership with the formation of both the West Somerset Railway Company and the West Somerset Railway Association (the volunteer support group) towards the eventual reopening of the first section between Minehead and Blue Anchor on 28 March 1976. The line was reopened in stages until being fully open to Bishops Lydeard in June 1979. Full restoration through to Taunton had remained a distant dream following firstly political difficulties involving the Unions and then the very high costs of rebuilding the line between Norton Fitzwarren and Taunton, following modernisation of the main line and signalling through the county town.

The WSR has slowly developed into one of the country's leading preserved railways, now carrying around 200,000 passengers per annum and indirectly contributing an estimated £6m to the local economy. It employs around 30 full time staff and over 200 volunteers.

The railway runs regular steam (and some diesel) services between Bishops Lydeard and Minehead between March and October each year plus a shorter period in December. The 3 miles of track between Bishops Lydeard and Norton Fitzwarren, linking the line to the mainline network, remain available for occasional use by WSR services at special gala weekends, and indeed a limited number of diesel-railcar-operated trains do run over the section in the off peak season. This link also enables the railway to host through excursion trains from around the UK, both steam and diesel hauled. It was also key to enabling the operation of heavy stone trains in connection with sea defence, and more recently road rebuilding works. It also allows the railway to provide for storage of rolling stock and training facilities to mainline train companies. A visit by H.R.H. the Duke of Edinburgh aboard the Royal Train also took place in 2002.

Today's West Somerset line starts at Bishops Lydeard Station, headquarters of the West Somerset Railway Association, with its museum displays and shop. The line immediately begins a 4 mile climb at a ruling gradient of 1 in 80 through some beautiful countryside to Crowcombe Heathfield, the summit of the line. There then follows a 6 mile descent through more fine Quantock scenery, passing the country halt at Stogumber, until Williton is reached, this being the halfway point on the journey and home of the Diesel and Electric Preservation Group's fleet. The line then continues on to meet the sea at Doniford before curving back inland at Watchet and climbing again to the village of Washford, today home of the Somerset & Dorset Railway Trust. A sharp descent at 1 in 65 down to the coast at Blue Anchor follows and then a run along the edge of the beach before the final 3 miles of mainly level track through Dunster and into Minehead, headquarters of the railway company and the location of the main loco sheds and workshops. The line is base for number of steam and diesel locomotives and rolling stock. It aims to capture the ambience of a busy GWR branch line and show some other historical features connected with the railways of the West Country in general. Its magnificently restored stations are a pleasure to visit and just sit and take in the atmosphere of a country station of times past. They also abound in railway infrastructure, such as signals and signal boxes, lamp huts and various trolleys etc, all things largely lost on the mainline network of today.

This book attempts to show the line in its full glory and show how it fits into the surrounding landscape so well. It is probably fair to say that the line consists of two halves – quiet countryside and bustling seaside. The undulating nature of the land around it, particularly on the Quantock half, allows for some very scenic landscape photography to be achieved with the train as the focal point. I have tried herein to show a mix of scenic-landscape-type views with some more traditional trains and railway pictures, and show some of the great variety of engines and trains that have worked over the line in recent years.

My photographic season is mostly between October and April, when the sun is lower in the sky and the light subsequently crisper. This allows the lower parts of the train to be highlighted and show up extra details, even from a medium distance viewpoint. During these months the cooler air also enables the exhaust of the steam locomotives to show up clearly and bring the picture to life, whilst in the warm air of summer it all but disappears, the only exception to this being in early morning or evening, and sometimes when near the coastal sections of the line. These months also mean that trains running in the late afternoon can be seen around sunset, producing some stunning glint effects – almost a holy grail for railway photographers!

Hopefully reading through the book will not only give you an idea of the multiplicity of trains that can be seen running on the WSR but inspire you to visit the line, if you have not already, and perhaps try your hand at some photography in the wonderful countryside around the line. If you do decide to try some photography yourself though, please do bear in mind that trespass on the railways property is not only illegal but can be dangerous and should only be attempted when in possession of a lineside pass, available from the Railway Company at Minehead, and following some safety advice. Also please respect local landowners and do not trespass upon land without prior permission.

Don Bishop,
West Huntspill,
Feb 2005.

Further historical information on the WSR's line is available from a variety of books and West Somerset Railway – a view from the past *by Richard Jones, is a recommended read. I would like to acknowledge the use of that book for some of the historical references made in this introduction.*

MAP OF THE WSR

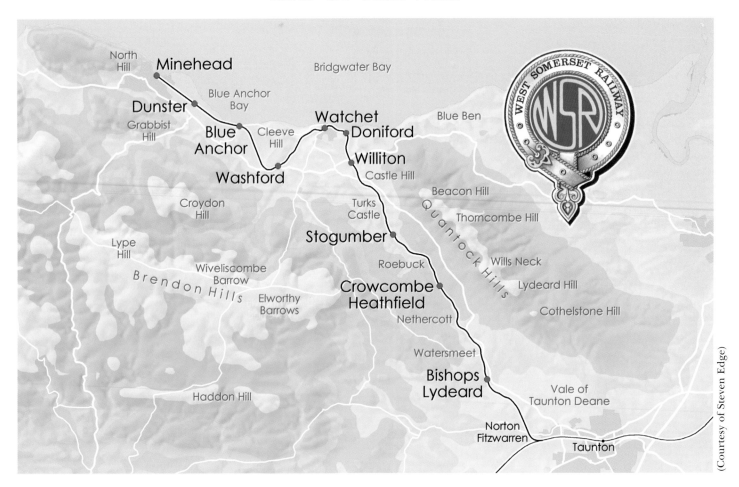

(Courtesy of Steven Edge)

The WSR at its best, new Mogul rebuild No. 9351 and Large Prairie No. 5199 crossing Ker Moor shortly after leaving Blue Anchor with the Bristol Channel seashore in the background. 30 September 2004.

Don Bishop collection/James Besley

It is June 1976, and a very different scene at Bishops Lydeard to that which we see today, with WSR train services yet to return. Stored awaiting restoration are, nearest the camera, small Prairie No. 5542, looking very derelict following over fifteen years in the Barry scrapyard, and sister loco No. 5521 – which was subsequently sold and is now undergoing restoration in the Forest of Dean – both having been purchased for restoration by the young West Somerset Railway Association in 1975.

And what we see today – No. 5542 in fully restored condition passes through Doniford Beach Halt in April 2003. The loco was restored by the separate 5542 Loco Group following purchase from the WSRA and was returned to service in 2002.

CLASSIC WSR

Left: For almost ten years Manor 4-6-0s have been the staple motive power on the WSR, and No. 7828 Odney Manor is seen passing over the rooftops at Nethercott with the 16.05 Bishops Lydeard – Minehead service on 5 May 1996.

Right: The line's other resident Manor – No. 7820 Dinmore Manor – blows off surplus steam as it climbs past Bye Farm with a Minehead-bound service on 31 March 1997.

Large Prairie No. 4141 rounds the curve from Leigh Woods with a Minehead to Bishops Lydeard service, which includes the Quantock Belle stock, on 30 March 2003. This loco is owned by Dr John Kennedy and currently resides at the Great Central Railway in Loughborough.

Pete Waterman's small Prairie No. 5553 at Nethercott with a Bishops Lydeard – Minehead train on 4 October 2003. This recently restored loco is based at Crewe and is a frequent visitor to the WSR.

A regular performer on the WSR is BR Standard tank No. 80136 which here works away from Doniford Halt at Liddymore with the 10.15 Minehead to Bishops Lydeard on 28 April 2001.

No. 5553 working a train up the little used section of line between Norton Fitzwarren and Bishops Lydeard with a photo charter consisting of a GW Siphon van and two coaches on 2 January 2004. The 3 miles between Bishops Lydeard and Norton Fitzwarren provide the WSR with its mainline link but is not used for regular steam hauled services. However with future developments planned by the railway at Norton Fitzwarren this situation may change.

South Devon Railway-based Hall 4-6-0 No. 4920 Dumbleton Hall working a Minehead-bound train past Kentsford near Watchet on 12 April 1997. This loco spent two years on the WSR before the expiry of its ten-yearly boiler ticket in 1998.

A lovely view of the 17.30 Minehead to Bishops Lydeard train on 27 August 1994 leaving Williton behind S & D 2-8-0 No. 88. The Bristol Channel and distant Welsh coastline are visible behind.

DOUBLEHEADED

Visiting 57xx class Panniers No. 5786 (from the South Devon Railway) and 5764 (from the Severn Valley Railway) doublehead an afternoon Minehead to Bishops Lydeard train out of Blue Anchor during the Spring gala weekend on 30 March 2003.

Opposite: 138 ton Peak diesel No. D120 pilots WSR based class 25 No. D7523 up the final few yards of Washford Bank's 1 in 65 gradient with a Bishops Lydeard-bound train on 4 May 1996. D120 spent most of 1996 working trains on the WSR following its loan for a diesel gala weekend; at one stage it became the only working diesel loco on the line following a spate of failures.

During the 1990s Collett 0-6-0 No. 3205 spent a number years based on the WSR and following an overhaul re-entered traffic for the Spring gala in 1997. Here the engine doubleheads No. 7820 Dinmore Manor past Bye Farm with a Williton to Minehead service as one of its first runs on 21 March 1997.

WSR-based BR blue diesel hydraulics, Western No. D1010 Western Campaigner (then running as D1035 Western Yeoman) and Hymek No. D7017 round Roebuck Curve with the 13.50 Bishops Lydeard – Minehead on 13 May 1995.

Swanage Railway-based Southern M7 0-4-4T No. 30053 visited the WSR for the 2003 Spring branch-line gala weekend and is seen here doubleheading resident GW large Prairie No. 4160 downhill near Leigh Woods crossing on 30 March 2003.

Opposite: A scene that could be on the infamous banks of the South Devon mainline – Manor No. 7820 Dinmore Manor and Castle No. 5051 Earl Bathurst head a charter special around the sharply curved and graded section of line at Churchlands near Nethercott in March 2000.

The WSR's new design of small boilered GW Mogul No. 9351 entered traffic for the first time at the 2004 Autumn gala. The loco was formerly Swindon-built large Prairie No. 5193 and was converted to a tender engine for operating convenience by the WSR using a design drawn up, but never built, by the GWR. Its number lent itself to rearrangement thus falling into line with what would quite probably have been its GW number as all GW 2-6-0 Mogul locos had a 3 as the second digit of their number. Here the newly outshopped loco climbs past Nethercott doubleheading one its former sisters – large Prairie No. 5199 with a Minehead-bound train on 30 September 2004.

An attempt to recreate a scene from the old Cambrian routes of Wales with a photo charter on 13 May 1996, and a dramatic start away from Bishops Lydeard by Manors No. 7820 Dinmore Manor and 7828 Odney Manor.

PHOTOCHARTERS

The West Somerset Railway Association-owned GW small Prairie No. 4561 is a personal favourite of mine, as I was involved with its initial restoration at Minehead in 1988/89. At 08.00 hrs on 20 March 1997 the by then work-worn loco is seen passing through Bishops Lydeard station with two ex GW coaches, which had been loaned to the WSR by the Severn Valley Railway for use during the filming of 'The Land Girls' feature film. The coaches stayed on for the 1997 Spring gala. They are also seen at Roebuck in the beautiful Spring lighting that morning.

For the first of what has now become a well established 'must visit' event in many enthusiasts diaries – the WSR Spring gala weekend – a Somerset & Dorset theme was employed using a number of the larger locomotives of types that worked over the famous former route between Bath and Bournemouth to recreate some long lost scenes. These types had never before been seen on the WSR. One of a number of photo charters also run around that time was on 1 April 1996 using Bulleid 4-6-2 No. 34039 Boscastle. Here the charter is seen crossing Ker Moor with Dunster Castle in the background – a rare shot to get correctly lit, only possible at certain times of the year early in the morning.

A Western Region express recreation. Manor No. 7820 Dinmore Manor and Castle No. 5051 Earl Bathurst are seen climbing hard past Nethercott on 21 March 2000. No. 5051 is owned by the Great Western Society and normally based at Didcot from where it occasionally works mainline tours, including to Minehead on some occasions for WSR gala events.

BR Standard tank No. 80136, built at Brighton in 1956, was initially restored by its owners for use at the Churnet Valley Railway in Staffordshire, but has spent a number of recent years based on the WSR. On 8 April 2002 the engine was used to recreate a typical 1960's mixed passenger and perishables train of the old North Cornwall lines of the LSWR system. It is seen here passing Sampford Brett early that morning.

On 3 May 1994 Severn Valley-based Standard 4 4-6-0 No. 75069, which was visiting for that season, passes the site of the Leigh Bridge loop signal box, working downhill, with a mixed parcels van train.

Probably the most popular photo charters are those involving goods trains and a typical mixed goods train, including a number of engineers wagons, is being hauled past Castle Hill by S & D 2-8-0 No. 88 as the Autumn colours start to appear on 25 October 1993.

A very unusual visitor to the WSR in 2004 was Great Eastern J15 0-6-0 No. 65462 from the North Norfolk Railway. The opportunity was taken to match it with the WSR's mixed heritage goods train on 22 March, seen here passing Castle Hill near Williton that afternoon on its way to Bishops Lydeard.

A further view of the J15 hauled goods, seen here glinting in the late afternoon sun as it rounds Roebuck Curve. This veteran from East London's Stratford works in 1912, proved only capable of hauling the lightest of trains over the WSR's steep gradients.

Another charter using the Railway's newly overhauled goods train was on 23 March 2004, this time recreating a typical Minehead branch goods train using small Prairie No. 5552 from the Bodmin Railway. Here the train is passing Castle Hill viewed from a more unusual angle across the nearby Doniford stream.

Bodmin's No. 5552 is seen passing Bicknoller with its goods train on 23 March 2004. This engine is one of four 55xx class locomotives recently restored and working back in their old stamping ground of the West Country, recreating a situation of some fifty years ago.

With one of the first photo charters to run on the WSR, large Prairie tank No. 4160 is silhouetted against the setting sun of 20 November 1993, as it passes Watersmeet near Bishops Lydeard with a mixed goods train.

SMALL PRAIRIES

GW 55xx tank No. 5553 has been West Somerset Railway-based regularly in recent years and is seen climbing up from Bishops Lydeard at Nethercott with a Winter gala service on 28 December 2003. No. 5553 was the last locomotive to leave the famous Barry scrapyards and was restored privately in the Midlands before being sold to its current owner Pete Waterman.

Opposite: On 5 May 1996 it was necessary to work an additional Minehead to Bishops Lydeard service at short notice due to increased passenger numbers, and here the additional 18.35 from Minehead is seen rounding Roebuck Curve behind No. 4561. This loco is currently stored out of use in the Gauge Museum at Bishops Lydeard, awaiting funding for a full overhaul to commence.

Low winter lighting casts deep shadows across Watchet Station as 4561 arrives with a Minehead to Bishops Lydeard working in December 1989. At this time the WSR's DMU fleet had been temporarily withdrawn for asbestos checks and steam was substituted for a short while on the local winter services. These trains are no longer operated by the WSR.

The Dean Forest Railway has 55xx tank No. 5541 based on its line and has kindly loaned the engine to the WSR on several occasions. Here it is seen passing Bicknoller with the 14.15 ex Minehead service on 19 March 1999.

Viewed from the hillside across the Doniford stream, approaching Williton is No. 4561 with the 10.15 Minehead to Bishops Lydeard train on 19 March 1995. This 45xx tank is one of the variety with smaller straight topped water tanks as opposed to the slightly larger sloped top tanks of the 55xx group.

The then recently restored 55xx tank No. 5542, an old regular of the Minehead branch in both GWR and BR days – being based at Taunton shed – approaches Roebuck crossing with a Bishops Lydeard-bound train on 28 December 2002 against a dark threatening sky. This engine passed the million miles of service mark during the 2003 season.

THE MANORS

The first Manor 4-6-0 to work over the line in the preservation era was the Severn Valley Railway-based No. 7802 Bradley Manor which visited the line in 1994 for a period of running in. The engine is seen at Castle Hill, Williton during that period with the 17.30 ex Minehead on 1 August 1995.

No. 7802 again, this time leaving Stogumber with the 10.15 Minehead to Bishops Lydeard on 17 September 1994, during that year's Autumn gala weekend.

Such was the success of No. 7802's visit that the WSR decided to hire No. 7828 Odney Manor from owner Ken Ryder for the 1995 season. The engine subsequently remained based on the WSR being ideally suited to the line's gradients and traffic requirements. It is seen here passing Combe Florey with a Minehead-bound train in December 2001 with Bagborough Hill in the Quantocks as a backdrop.

In 2004 7828's owner Ken Ryder decided to sell the engine, as it was now due an expensive ten yearly overhaul, and the engine passed into the ownership of the West Somerset Railway Plc. Funds are now being sought to overhaul the engine for at least another ten years of regular use on the WSR. No. 7828 storms uphill at Nethercott on 22 December 2001.

No. 7820 Dinmore Manor had arrived originally on the WSR in ex scrapyard condition from the Gwili Railway near Carmarthen in the late 1980s. It was then taken to Tyseley Works in Birmingham for full restoration by its owning group and returned to the WSR to enter traffic in 1995. The engine became a regular on the line for the next nine years until withdrawal for a further overhaul in 2004. On 31 March 1997 it worked downhill at Roebuck Curve, by special request, with a Minehead-bound train.

The Manors were designed by the GWR for use on routes with a lighter axle loading and for piloting duties. They were common over the famous Devon banks between Newton Abbot and Plymouth and on the former Cambrian routes of Wales. After the war a need was established for further locomotives of this type by the then nationalised British Railways Board and so Swindon Works turned out Nos. 7820–7829 in 1950. Both WSR based Manors are from this BR-built batch. In December 1999 No. 7820 was the rostered engine for the Santa Special trains between Bishops Lydeard and Crowcombe Heathfield and is seen here climbing past Churchlands.

Further Santa Special action as 7828 Odney Manor storms uphill at Churchlands Bridge, Combe Florey on 8 December 2001 with strong backlighting only seen in deep winter and possible with the first train of the day at this location.

WINTER

The WSR's new Mogul No. 9351 saw its first season of 'Santa duties' in 2004 and was then subsequently used in the Christmas holiday week for a private driver experience charter on 28 December. It leaves Bishops Lydeard just after sunrise that morning bound for Minehead.

Opposite: An additional empty coaching stock (ecs) movement was required to enable a charter train to operate to Minehead and back for a private party on 15 December 2001. This presented an excellent additional photo opportunity which was greeted with bright sunny conditions as Standard tank No. 80136 approached Crowcombe with the ecs train.

A pleasant picture opportunity available with relative ease in December/January each year is at Bishops Lydeard Station for the first of the day's trains. Strong backlighting produces a pleasant golden effect on 1 January 1995 as the well known Bishops Lydeard shop manager, John Pearce, discusses the news with the crew of No. 4561.

Fog is of course a very difficult weather condition in which to take any decent pictures. However, if you are lucky enough to find a train just as the sun burns the fog away a very pleasant result can be obtained. Although running bunker first, I caught WSRA-owned Pannier No. 6412 in such conditions at Crowcombe on 1 January 1993 with the 11.50 ex Bishops Lydeard train.

The last of the afternoon's Santa trains from Bishops Lydeard is a difficult one to catch in sunlight. However, in 1997 it ran at 15.20 rather than the usual 15.25 from Bishops Lydeard – the extra five minutes made all the difference for a nice shot just as the sun set and lit the engine's exhaust from underneath to produce a nice orange glow. Collett 0-6-0 No. 3205 passes Watersmeet on 14 December 1997.

The Christmas holiday week of 2001 was quite memorable for producing some lovely cold sunny weather for the full week. The WSR's Christmas week services that year were worked by Std 4 tank No. 80136. Here the 14.25 ex Minehead appears at Roebuck Curve on 29 December 2001.

A scene which could quite easily be in the 1960s 'change over period' from steam to diesel traction on many branch lines. 55xx No. 5553 approaches Bishops Lydeard from the Norton Fitzwarren direction as a DMU is passed on the former up line (now part of the WSR's storage sidings) to create this passing trains image early on 2 January 2004.

INTO SPRING

The pleasant mix of colours that signify Spring, are seen in abundance at Bilbrook as No. 80136 climbs up Washford Bank with the 10.15 Minehead to Bishops Lydeard on 28 April 2001.

Before the trees have gone into full leaf in the early Spring, some very pleasant and colourful shots can be obtained. WSR-based large Prairie No. 4160 passes Nornvis Bridge on its way up to Crowcombe with the 16.05 ex Bishops Lydeard in April 2002. No. 4160 was restored by volunteers at Minehead, entered traffic in 1993 and proved a popular and capable engine for the WSR's needs. It was withdrawn for overhaul in 2003 and is expected to return to traffic in 2005.

Opposite: Early evening light greets Hall class No. 4920 Dumbleton Hall as it departs from Blue Anchor along the beach with the 17.30 ex Bishops Lydeard on 31 March 1997. Storms during the past winter had caused the sand banks visible behind the train to cover the old lineside fences and so for a short while the line appeared unfenced at this location.

Severn Valley Railway-based GW Mogul No. 7325 passes Bye Farm with the 14.30 Bishops Lydeard to Minehead on 19 March 1999. This engine is one of a type that regularly worked trains over the Minehead branch in BR days, particularly on busy Summer Saturdays. It visited the WSR on three occasions in the late 1990s before withdrawal for a full overhaul.

SUMMER

The WSR usually hires at least one guest engine in for each main running season to help cover its services with the home based fleet: in 1996 this was ex GW 2-8-0T No. 4277. This large tank design was built mainly for use on heavy coal trains in the South Wales Valleys. On withdrawal in 1964 it went to Barry scrapyard where it remained until private purchase in 1986. It is currently awaiting an overhaul near Swindon. No. 4277 is seen working the 17.48 Bishops Lydeard to Minehead train past Nethercott on 23 August 1996 .

For the 2002 season, another of the ex GW 2-8-0 tanks visited the WSR, this time No. 5224, now owned by TV personality Pete Waterman and nominally based at Crewe. No. 5224 is painted in the later BR unlined black livery carried by the class after nationalisation, and on 7 September 2002 passed Bicknoller with a Minehead to Bishops Lydeard train which included some of the Quantock Belle dining stock.

Another predominantly goods engine to visit the WSR was LMS 8F No. 48773 from the Severn Valley Railway, which spent most of 1993 based on the line. The 8F is seen here drifting downhill past Combe Florey with the 17.30 ex Minehead service on 30 August 1993. The engine has a long historical pedigree as a wartime workhorse, including a period of service in Egypt.

Possibly one of the most famous trains of recent times, with the younger generation at least, is the 'Hogwarts Express' of Harry Potter fame. The first locomotive to carry the distinctive red livery for publicity purposes was Bulleid West Country class No. 34027 Taw Valley. After its promotional work for the film makers was over, the loco moved to the WSR for the main summer season in 2000. The WSR was able to get permission to run the loco with its Hogwarts Express nameplates during this visit and it proved very popular with our younger visitors. The fictionally-liveried red loco is seen topping the climb of Washford Bank with a Minehead to Bishops Lydeard train in August 2000.

AUTUMN

From 2003 it was decided to move the Autumn Gala weekend back a few weeks to the first weekend of October to ease the pressure on the operating departments after the main summer season. This does mean that the autumn colours are starting to appear during the event. Amid some early Autumn hues on 4 October 2003 WSRA Pannier No. 6412 leaves Stogumber with the beautifully restored GW Autocoach No. 178 on an early morning Minehead to Bishops Lydeard working.

Another view of one of the first photo charters organised on the WSR on 20 November 1993 (see page 33), with large Prairie No. 4160 and short goods train. That day was blessed with some stunning Autumn weather with early morning frost and mists. The exhaust hangs in the still cold air as No. 4160 climbs away from Bishops Lydeard at Watersmeet.

As the leaves start to drop from the trees on 26 October 2004 the WSR's new Mogul No. 9351 emerges from the small copse at Nethercott with the 16.05 ex Bishops Lydeard to Minehead.

The Llangollen Railway kindly loaned the WSR its recently restored large Prairie No. 5199 for the Autumn 2004 gala, and the loco was used for a photo charter on 4 October with the railway's demonstration goods train. An advantage of photo charters is that you can arrange for a loco to 'work' downhill to produce steam effects at locations where this would not normally be possible on service trains, such as here at Stones Woods near Crowcombe.

THE 9Fs

Another visiting engine for the Autumn 2004 gala was 9F 2-10-0 No. 92214 from the Midland Railway Centre in Derbyshire. This was the third 9F to work on the WSR and was only recently restored by its owning group. Hopefully the engine will make a repeat visit in the near future for an S & D gala weekend. The 9F is seen here climbing through Stones Wood towards Crowcombe with the 12.15 ex Minehead service on 2 October 2004.

Undoubtedly the star of the 1980s on the WSR – 9F 2-10-0 No. 92220 Evening Star, the last steam loco-motive built by British Railways, at Swindon in March 1960 – visited the line from the National Railway Museum, York for the 1989 season. The WSR had just turned the corner after a number of years of uncertainty and financial struggles and the visit of such a famous and prestigious loco as Evening Star firmly established the WSR among the top preserved lines in the UK. The loco was often used that year for additional charter workings, sometimes loading to 12 coaches. No. 92220 is passing the well known spot at Castle Hill near Williton with a Minehead to Bishops Lydeard train in April 1989 .

The 9Fs were the most successful of the BR standard designs, which numbered 999 locos in all; building of the 251 engines commenced in 1954 and ended with 92220 in March 1960. Some of the locos in the class only saw five or six year's service before withdrawal as dieselisation took place rapidly. Another of the survivors is No. 92212 which was restored at the Great Central Railway, but now resides at the Mid Hants Railway. This loco visited the WSR for the Spring 2003 gala and works away from Stogumber on 24 March 2003 with the Quantock Belle stock on a Bishops Lydeard-bound working.

The very popular No. 92214 works onto the curve at Roebuck Farm on its way to Bishops Lydeard on 19 September 2004. These powerful locos earned themselves an excellent reputation in BR service as free steaming and free running, capable of running up to 90 mph, although this was frowned upon by the authorities.

THE 7F

A locomotive with a long historical association with the railways of Somerset, is the Somerset & Dorset Railway 7F 2-8-0 No. 53808. This loco was part of a second batch of five of this class, which totalled 11 engines built exclusively to work trains over the heavily graded S & D route through the Mendip Hills between Bath and Evercreech Junction and onto Bournemouth. The 1925 built engine was withdrawn from service in 1963 and was sent to Woodham's Barry scrapyard from where it was rescued by the Somerset & Dorset Railway Circle (later Trust) in 1970 and moved to their base at Radstock. Following the enforced closure of that site, such was the negative view of railway preservation in political circles in those days, the engine moved to the WSR for restoration. This was completed in 1987. Here the engine climbs past Eastcombe with the 10.25 ex Bishops Lydeard on 4 May 1996.

No. 53808 gave the WSR a good eight year's service before having to be withdrawn for a further full overhaul in May 1996. The engine was a popular performer throughout this time, particularly so in its correct BR black livery for the final two months of that period of service. Again on the 4 May 1996, the 7F is seen working downhill by special request, at Roebuck Curve, with the 17.45 ex Bishops Lydeard, and hauling the 16.00 Bishops Lydeard to Minehead train past Kentsford, Watchet, on 27 April 1996. The engine is due to return to traffic once again in 2005 following the overhaul which has cost around £350,000.

Whilst carrying its S & D black livery, No. 88 approaches Roebuck crossing at the head of the 14.25 from Minehead on 18 April 1995.

SOMERSET & DORSET RECREATIONS

As home to the 7F and the S & D Trust, the WSR has been keen to recreate scenes from the old S & D, and a major gala event with four visiting engines was held in March 1996 to commemorate thirty years since closure of the S & D route, and is to be repeated in 2006 (forty years!). In conditions typical of the Mendip Hills, but normally useless for good photography, a photo charter recreation climbs over Watersmeet Bridge hauled by the classic S & D combination of 7F No. 53807 (alias 53808) and un-rebuilt Bulleid Pacific No. 34105 Swanage on 15 March 1996.

The rebuilt Bulleid West Country class Pacific No. 34039 Boscastle from the Great Central Railway also took part in the 1996 event and was used for a photo charter on 1 April 1996, seen here climbing Washford Bank near Blue Anchor.

As a comparison to the rebuilt No. 34039, here is a view of original streamlined (un-rebuilt) Bulleid Pacific No. 34105 Swanage with a gala special working to commemorate thirty years since closure of the famous Bath to Bournemouth route, at Kentsford Farm crossing on 10 March 1996.

A popular feature of gala weekends is the running of a demonstration goods train and for the S & D – this just had to be behind the 7F. Specially renumbered to recreate one of its long-lost sister engines, 53806, the 7F climbs away from Bishops Lydeard at Eastcombe with its mixed goods on 10 March 1996.

Opposite: Another loco type closely associated with the S & D is the Midland 4F, and this particular member of the class spent much of its working life based on the line, so it was a must have for the organisers of the S & D event. The Churnet Valley Railway kindly allowed No. 44422 to visit the WSR for around two months in 1996 and the opportunity was taken for a photo charter on 31 March 1996, seen at Roebuck Curve amid flowering Spring gorse with the Quantock Belle set.

More recently the Spring 2004 gala weekend featured two engines of types that would have been seen over the S & D, so it was decided to run a doubleheaded train very much as they would have done on that line in BR days. The featured locos are BR Standard 4 2-6-0 No. 76079 and re-built West Country class No. 34045 Ottery St Mary (actually 34027 Taw Valley but renumbered by its owner in recent years), seen hammering past Kentsford crossing with a Bishops Lydeard to Minehead working on 26 March 2003.

DIESEL HYDRAULICS

Another aspect of the West Somerset Railway is that it is also home to a number of diesel locomotives, maintained by the Diesel & Electric Preservation Group Ltd from their base at Williton Station. The DEPG was set up in the 1970s to preserve a diesel hydraulic Hymek loco, a type that was being rendered extinct around that time by a BR standardisation plan which was to see all hydraulic transmission locomotives withdrawn and replaced by more standard diesel electric types. The group's first acquisition was Hymek D7017 and on 13 May 1995 the loco is seen working the 10.25 ex Bishops Lydeard past Cedar Falls. In time the group also purchased a second Hymek loco, No. D7018, which was initially based at Didcot in Oxfordshire. However the group's entire fleet was moved to Williton in 1990 and the WSR gained the services of a second Hymek. No. D7018 is seen hauling a two-coach 12.15 Minehead to Bishops Lydeard service away from Blue Anchor in place of a DMU on 10 October 1993.

The Western Region of BR had opted for hydraulic transmission for its new diesel fleet in the 1950/60s in typical GWR go it alone style. The hydraulics were deemed non standard and listed for replacement in the early 1970s despite their comparatively young age. In celebration of the diesel hydraulic era, the DEPG and WSR get together to organise special events to recreate this important period in West Country railway history. Other preserved diesel hydraulic locos are sometimes brought in for these events. The East Lancashire Railway (you couldn't get much further from their old stamping ground!) have sent several locos over the years, and Warship class No. D832 Onslaught from that railway glints as it appears at Roebuck Curve with an afternoon Bishops Lydeard-bound train at the 1995 diesel gala.

Many people will remember diesel locos as being often rather dirty, and this was particularly so for the diesel hydraulic types towards the end of their lives. With this in mind the DEPG specially painted their Western D1010 Western Campaigner in BR blue livery with artistically applied dirt, shown here passing Kentsford Farm on 28 March 1998 with the 12.00 ex Bishops Lydeard.

The diesel hydraulics are also used on some normal WSR services such as this evening service from Bishops Lydeard to Minehead with D7017 darkening the sky as it leaves Blue Anchor on 12 August 1998. Diesel traction is frequently used on the evening Fish and Chips specials from Bishops Lydeard.

Visiting diesel locos are usually brought to the WSR by a special rail movement. At Bishops Lydeard D1041 Western Prince and D832 Onslaught await collection for their return home to East Lancashire after the 1995 diesel hydraulic gala.

Late afternoon at Bye Farm on the climb to Washford can produce some lovely lighting effects, such as here when BR blue-liveried Warship D832 Onslaught passed with a Minehead-bound train in May 1995.

The WSR based Western D1010 Western Campaigner is currently painted maroon, the livery in which it was first outshopped from Swindon in 1962. Looking very smart in its new livery, then with yellow buffer beams, it is seen working a special past Bicknoller en route to Bishops Lydeard complete with headboard.

AUTOTRAINS

When the now WSR-based Autocoach No. 178 first arrived on the line the 5542 loco group decided to temporally equip their loco to work with the coach. On 28 December 2003 No. 5542 leads its Autocoach through Doniford Halt. Auto No. 178 is privately owned and visited the WSR for the Autumn 2003 gala weekend; subsequently agreement was reached for the coach to be based on the WSR and it attends most gala weekends. In between these events the coach is either stored under cover at Williton or away visiting other lines. The 5542 group has now purchased an Autocoach of their own which is in need of major restoration once fund raising efforts bear fruit.

Opposite: A very popular feature of recent WSR gala weekends has been the use of a GWR Autocoach in push pull formation with an appropriately equipped loco. The first appearance on the line of an Autotrain was in September 1996 when Collett 0-4-2T No. 1450 visited the line along with the South Devon Railway's Autocoach W228 in BR red & cream livery. The pair are seen from the farm track at Roebuck on the evening of 22 September 1996.

THE QUANTOCK BELLE

The WSR's visiting engine for the 1994 season was Standard class 4 4-6-0 No. 75069 and on 13 August 1994 it worked an evening Quantock Belle service past Cedar Falls. Many QB workings are on Saturday evenings throughout the Summer.

Opposite: The West Somerset Railway Association has invested in four vehicles which are used almost exclusively for dining trains, known as the Quantock Belle. This train is run entirely by a group of volunteers who dedicate a lot of their spare time to maintaining and staffing the train with profits being ploughed back into West Somerset Railway Association funds. The train normally runs on weekends throughout the Summer plus some special charter workings. On 30 March 2003 2-8-0T No. 5224 is seen passing Yarde Farm Bridge with a QB working during the Spring gala weekend.

MILK TRAINS

The WSR is home to a couple of six wheeled milk tanks, once a common sight on West Country lines. These tanks are popular for photographic charters along with an appropriate restored GW Siphon van. One such charter on 25 March 2003 employed No. 5542 for the day, and it is seen here looking very at home in the Great Western atmosphere of Crowcombe Heathfield Station.

Opposite: A good variety of visiting engines has been used on photo charters with the milk tanks in recent years and one such was Mid Hants Railway based Ivatt 2-6-2T No. 41312 in March 1999, here passing Roebuck Gate Farm with the two tanks and a BR maroon brake coach.

For the branch line event of March 2003 the line borrowed Swanage Railway-based M7 0-4-4T No. 30053. The opportunity was again taken to run a milk train charter and the train is seen passing Nethercott with the Quantock Hills as a backdrop on 4 April 2003.

Early morning mist and fog starts to clear at Roebuck on 17 March 1999 as Severn Valley-based Mogul No. 7325 passes with a milk train.

THE PHOENIX – NO. 71000

Possibly the biggest loco to visit the WSR so far was unique BR Class 8 Pacific No. 71000 Duke of Gloucester. The engine had worked down to Paignton on a railtour and had become stranded by the cancellation of its booked return run. The owners asked the WSR if they would provide a stabling facility for a few weeks and the WSR was only too pleased to oblige. At the time the WSR was just going through the final stages of getting formal approval to operate larger locos on the line. Once granted the opportunity was taken to use No. 71000 for a number of special runs and on certain service trains for a limited period. On 28 August 1995 the engine hauls the 14.20 Bishops Lydeard to Minehead at Cedar Falls.

Duke of Gloucester was built in 1954 to replace another locomotive written off in the terrible disaster at Harrow and Wealdstone, and was built to a unique design specification with Caprotti valve gear. It was not overly successful during its BR career at a time when dieselisation took priority and on withdrawal the cylinder block was kept back for the Science Museum and the rest of the loco sent for scrap. A quite interesting story then unfolded, too long to repeat here, which saw the remains of the loco saved for preservation despite most people thinking the group behind the scheme were all mad! Eventually they proved the sceptics wrong and the engine was restored to working order in 1986 and to mainline running a few years later, earning its 'Phoenix' title. Its performance was drastically improved following the discovery of design faults and it is arguably the most advanced steam engine ever to grace British tracks. On 27 August 1995 No. 71000 passes Kentsford with the 16.00 from Bishops Lydeard, and the following day leaves Bishops Lydeard against some strong backlighting at Whisky Trail crossing, with the 10.25 to Minehead. The loco returned to service for mainline specials again in 2004.

THE KING

A little later that month the King worked a number of WSR services as part of a mileage accumulation exercise. These included working Minehead to Williton shuttles such as the one depicted here passing Liddymore on 19 March 2000.

Opposite: A frequent visitor to WSR galas and events since its first appearance in 1997 has been Great Western King class 4-6-0 No. 6024 King Edward I. It has worked on and off the WSR several times on special trains and worked regular service trains on a number of occasions in between mainline runs. In Spring 2000 following some repairs carried out at the Mid Hants Railway No. 6024 arrived on the WSR for a period of running in before attending a gala weekend and then further mainline tours. During the running-in trials the engine runs downhill from Crowcombe with its support coach in tow. March 2000.

The engine's visit and need to accumulate some miles presented the opportunity to run a photo charter, to date the only such working to have taken place with this engine. On 22 March 2000 King Edward I is seen climbing away from Bishops Lydeard at Whisky Trail crossing, so named because American GIs stationed in the area used the crossing during the Second World War to carry back supplies of whisky to their barracks.

The King class was designed and built by the GWR at Swindon commencing in 1927, and at the time was the most powerful loco to be introduced to service in the UK. The class spent some thirty-five years working expresses between London Paddington, the West Country, Bristol and Birmingham until withdrawal by BR in 1962 and replacement by new Western diesel hydraulics (see page 77). A further view from the Spring 2000 visit, this time approaching Blue Anchor Station with a Minehead to Williton working. 19 March 2000.

THROUGH TRAINS

Around half a dozen through diesel-hauled excursions run each year, and this may increase in coming years with the junction upgrade at Norton Fitzwarren. On 18 April 1998 Rail Express Systems (RES) liveried Class 47 No. 47763 approaches Blue Anchor heading for Minehead with an excursion from Wrexham. In more recent years regular railtour operator, EWS, has used its Type 5 freight diesels such this Class 66 No. 66132, working a Hertfordshire Railtours special past Bicknoller returning to the Home Counties from Minehead with a full set of Southern Region-style green Mk1 stock. Diesels from classes 31, 33, 37, 45, 47 and 56 have all worked trains onto the WSR.

Having a connection to the mainline network, which is due to be further upgraded in 2005, has enabled the WSR to host a number of through excursions from various parts of the country – hauled by both diesel and steam traction. A further visit by No. 6024 in 2001 ended on 19 May 2001 with a Minehead to Paddington train, hauled by No. 6024 from Minehead and joined by Castle No. 5029 Nunney Castle at Bristol, which had also been on the WSR around this time and worked ahead light engine for operational convenience. Unfortunately the King failed at Swindon with a hot axle box and the Castle continued onto London alone, entertaining the passengers to a blistering run up the fast mainline non stop all the way from Swindon to Paddington. The 06.30 Minehead to Paddington train approaches Crowcombe with No. 6024 working hard with 13 coaches in tow.

One of the earliest through trains to work on the WSR was this Hull – Minehead and return working on 13 April 1991 which utilised a Mk1 set owned by the Scottish Railway Preservation Society, and at that time in a variety of liveries – including some vehicles in different colours on each side! The tour ran into a number of problems en route to the WSR and eventually arrived over two hours late! The heavy train was worked on the WSR by the S & D 7F No. 53808 and here approaches Blue Anchor on its long return journey home.

Opposite: A major development for the WSR was its ability to show its full worth to the local community when between March 1997 to June 1998 it was used to convey over 105,000 tons of huge rock boulders to Minehead as part of the sea defence improvements carried out following severe flooding a few years before. Rather than put hundreds of heavy lorries onto Somerset's roads it was decided to use rail to convey the stone from the Mendip quarries through to Minehead using the WSR. Most trains were worked on the WSR by Class 37 diesels and here mainline blue-liveried No. 37798 approaches Williton on 15 April 1997 with a 13.34 Whatley Quarry to Minehead working.

STONE TRAINS

On a few occasions the stone trains were assisted on the Minehead branch section of their journey by WSR locos, either due to failure or operational difficulties; steam locos 1450 and 4160 were used along with Western D1010. On 30 March 1998 it was required to work diminutive 0-4-2T No. 1450 from Bishops Lydeard to Williton, and to save a separate 'train path' having to be found it was decided to work the engine down on the front of that day's stone train. Here approaching Crowcombe at Nornvis Bridge No. 1450 pilots Class 37 No. 37885 with its 528-ton train – readers can be assured that No. 1450 was not doing most of the work!

A second stone contract arose in Spring 2000 in conjunction with sea defence works at Doniford, which included protecting the WSR itself on the cliff tops at that location. A smaller amount of stone was required and it was handled by seven trains in March 2000. By this time many Class 37s had been withdrawn from service and more modern air-braked wagons were used with the result that newer class 59 and 66 locos were employed. Indeed the trains brought a few rare workings of members of the 59/2 sub class to the West Country. On 10 March 2000 No. 59206 is seen taking the empties back to the Mendip quarry past Combe Florey.

GOODS TRAINS

Traditional goods trains, as would have been seen many years ago, are more the norm on the WSR for a variety of reasons. Part of the WSR's driver experience programme, where you can buy a day's footplate experience driving and firing steam engines on the line, involves running special goods trains, and on 24 March 1993 Collett 0-6-0 No. 3205 drops downhill past Castle Hill towards Williton with such a working.

A regular feature of the gala weekends are shunting demonstrations at Dunster yard using a variety of engines – usually a smaller or spare engine from the day's passenger traffic. On 7 September 2002 small Prairie No. 5553 shunts the two milk tanks in Dunster yard.

A one off event, to date at least, was the running of a special wartime-style goods train for a 'railways and the war' weekend on 8 May 1994. The train conveyed a number of flat bed wagons loaded onto which were tanks and other military vehicles, hauled by the 7F No. 53808. Early that morning the 7F rounds Roebuck Curve with its heavy train.

Recently a group has been formed with the aim of restoring a number of the line's goods wagon fleet for exclusive use in a heritage goods train for demonstration purposes. On 24 October 2004 a 12 wagon rake is approaching Williton forming an early morning goods from Minehead behind No. 5542.

As part of the 1996 Somerset & Dorset event it was decided to run a short milk train early in the morning from Minehead, a traditional traffic type on the old S & D route. The Midland 4F 0-6-0 No. 44422 was employed for this task and on 9 March 1996 the 4F makes a wonderful sight climbing Washford Bank at Black Monkey Bridge with snow on the distant Brendon Hills behind.

Opposite: A locomotive type designed for hauling heavy goods trains was the GW 42xx 2-8-0T. On 16 September 2001 No. 4247, which visited the WSR for part of that season, has just passed Stogumber with a Minehead to Bishops Lydeard goods working.

WSR 2-8-0s AT WORK

The day-to-day trains on the line can often produce some of the best photographs, particularly I feel in the lighting of a Spring afternoon in April and May. One such occasion was on 4 May 1996 when 7F No. 53808 worked past Bye Farm with the 17.45 ex Bishops Lydeard.

The 1992 summer visitor to the line was the Great Western Society's Didcot-based GW heavy freight 2-8-0 No. 3822. The impressive machine passes Kentsford crossing on 20 April 1992 with a Bishops Lydeard to Minehead train. During this visit a special evening train was run to test the ability of No. 3822. The loco successfully hauled a 19-coach train the entire length of the line, including pulling away from a standing start on the 1 in 65 of Washford Bank following a brief stall.

SNOW

Over fifteen years of photographing the WSR's trains one weather condition that had evaded me was that of lying snow at the lineside with trains running, that kind of weather seemingly becoming rarer with each passing year – a result of global warming they say! However over the Christmas holiday week in 2000 my prayers were answered as snow fell over three nights and produced stunning conditions under clear blue skies on each of the following days. Crowcombe Station looks a real Christmas card scene on 28 December 2000 before the first of the day's trains appeared.

The winter peace of Roebuck is disturbed on 30 December 2000 as No. 7820 Dinmore Manor heads tender first with the 10.15 ex Minehead.

With the Bristol Channel and distant snow-covered Welsh hills behind, Dinmore Manor runs along the seashore at Blue Anchor with 12.25 ex Bishops Lydeard on 29 December 2000. The salty sea air around here ensures that snow is an even rarer event!

Opposite: Probably the most stunning picture I have taken on the WSR – with 3 inches of crisp snow lying all around, clear azure blue sky and cold still air, No. 7820 Dinmore Manor storms uphill at Churchlands with the 12.25 Bishops Lydeard to Minehead on 29 December 2000.

AT NIGHT

At night the railway takes on a whole new atmosphere and with special lighting set up some quite different images can be obtained. At Crowcombe Heathfield on 7 September 2002 is No. 4160 with a passenger formation.

The Dean Forest Railway's small Prairie No. 5541 stands outside Dunster goods shed during a gala evening photo shoot in September 1999.

Looking more like a mainline terminus than the end of a 23 mile branch line, King Class No. 6024 King Edward I stands in the main platform at Minehead on 25 March 2000 with an evening Quantock Belle working.

Hymeks D7017 and D7018 stand in Minehead station at the end of a day's diesel gala workings on 31 October 1992. At the time D7017 sported a fictitious 'Dutch' engineers-livery of grey and yellow and had snowploughs fitted, whilst D7018 was in a more realistic two-tone green livery.

Minehead shed on 25 March 2000. A special night photo shoot took place which featured several locomotives after they had completed their day's gala workings – outside the original goods shed was SVR-based Mogul No. 7325. This building was converted to a locomotive workshop by the WSR in the late 1970s and a new extension, seen alongside No. 7325, was completed in 1999.

Also present were Manors No. 7820 Dinmore Manor and 7828 Odney Manor, posed outside the new shed for the assembled photographers, they provided an almost timeless scene of an engine shed at night.

THE STANDARD TANK

A regular and popular performer in recent years has been the 1956 Brighton-built BR Standard tank No. 80136. On 22 December 2001 it was chartered for a day's private footplate experience and is seen leaving Blue Anchor and heading towards Williton.

A new innovation in 2001 was the introduction of a Williton to Blue Anchor Santa Special working to ease the pressure on other services. This meant it became possible to photograph a train climbing Washford Bank during the 'Santa season', previously not possible. On 23 December 2001 No. 80136 climbs the bank near Black Monkey Bridge with its return Williton-bound train.

The Quantock Hills provide a fine and colourful backdrop to this scene of No. 80136 climbing past the hamlet of Woolston on 31 December 2004 with the 14.25 ex Minehead service.

GALA VISITORS

As mentioned earlier in this book a great variety of visiting engines is brought onto the WSR for its special gala weekends. The first Castle Class 4-6-0 to run on the line was No. 7029 Clun Castle in March 1997, seen here passing Cedar Falls with the 09.25 Bishops Lydeard to Minehead service. Its train was formed mostly of ex DMU TCL vehicles in red and cream livery. These vehicles now only see limited use on WSR services and most have been repainted in chocolate and cream livery.

The railway also decided to hire in two ex GWR coaches from the Severn Valley Railway again for the Spring 2000 event following their popularity in 1997 (see page 24). On this occasion the two vintage coaches are seen passing Combe Florey behind large GW Prairie No. 4160, creating a scene typical of the Minehead branch in the late 1940s.

Later the same day the WSRA's Pannier No. 6412 was employed on a Minehead to Williton shuttle working using the two vintage GW vehicles, and approaches Williton at Liddymore Bridge, 25 March 2000.

A very small ex GWR engine that has visited many preserved lines in recent years has been SVR-based 0-6-0 saddle tank No. 813. It visited the WSR's Autumn 2001 gala and was employed for an early morning train formed of a single coach and a milk tank on 16 September 2001, seen passing the pretty Stogumber Station.

Three Castle's have worked on the line, the most frequent of these being 1934 built No. 5051 Earl Bathurst from Didcot. In March 2000 No. 5051 is seen passing Bye Farm with a Bishops Lydeard to Minehead service.

Opposite: Another type of loco built by the GWR for its extensive system of lines in South Wales was the 56xx class 0-6-2T. The only representative to have worked on the WSR to date is No. 5637, which is normally based at the East Somerset Railway at Cranmore near Shepton Mallet. On 4 October 2003 No. 5637 drifts past Water Farm near Stogumber against a stormy sky with a Minehead-bound service.

A very famous visitor, GW 4-4-0 No. 3440 City of Truro, the first engine to have reputedly reached 100 mph, when in May 1904, working an Ocean Mails special from Plymouth to London down Wellington Bank, it was timed at 102.6 mph. A feat that has been questioned many times over the years – particularly by enthusiasts of the LNER who believe that Flying Scotsman holds this title! Either way it earned this remarkable engine a place in railway history and preservation at the National Railway Museum. No. 3440 visited the line in 1992 and again for the very successful spring 2005 'Pride of the Great Western' gala. It is seen passing Roebuck Crossing with a Bishops Lydeard-bound train on the 18 March 2005.

A number of the recent Spring galas have been themed around branch lines of the West Country, and have seen a variety of appropriate motive power pay a visit. In 2003 the Swanage Railway-based M7 0-4-4T No. 30053 visited and is seen climbing away from Blue Anchor late on the 30 March with a Bishops Lydeard-bound train.

In contrast with the late afternoon shot opposite, is South Devon Railway-based 57xx Class Pannier tank No. 5786 passing Leigh Woods at 08.30 am on 29 March 2003. Visitors to the gala weekends often appreciate these early morning departures, particularly when staying in the area overnight.

Another early morning scene, this time featuring Panniers 6412 & 5764 as they lift the first Minehead to Bishops Lydeard service of the day away from Blue Anchor with Minehead and North Hill as a backdrop on 30 March 2003.

IN SILHOUETTE

A different type of railway photograph can be obtained by placing the train in front of the setting sun to produce a silhouette. On 25 May 1992 an 'Exmoor Diner' working from Minehead to Bishops Lydeard climbs Washford Bank behind Pannier No. 6412 as the sun sets over the Brendon Hills beyond.

Opposite: The best time of year to attempt a silhouette picture is deep winter, and on Boxing day 1993 Prairie No. 4160 departs Bishops Lydeard at Cedar Falls with a Minehead-bound train.

At the end of a day's photography with a milk train formation, hauled by visiting Ivatt 2-6-2T No. 41312, the train runs past Watersmeet on 18 March 1999.

CAPTURING THE GLINT

A 'Holy Grail' for railway photographers is getting a master shot in either early morning or evening lighting with a glint of the low sun reflected off the train. On 8 September 2002 No. 6024 King Edward I drifts towards Blue Anchor with a late afternoon Minehead to Bishops Lydeard service.

Probably the best location to get a glint on the WSR is along the beach at Blue Anchor on a July/August evening when the sun sets out over the sea to the north west of the line. Evening services such as the Quantock Belle and Sunset Special are the favourites. In August 2000 a special Bishops Lydeard to Minehead working, in conjunction with the WSRA's Bishops Lydeard steam rally, leaves Blue Anchor into the setting sun behind Manors 7820 Dinmore Manor and 7828 Odney Manor.

You need to position the sun at an angle of approx 45 degrees to the angle of your planned shot to get a glint unless you aim for a side on shot in which case you will be square on with the sun behind you. Here 7F No. 88 reflects gold as it passes Leigh Woods with its charter goods working on 25 October 1993.

Back on Blue Anchor beach, this time on 5 July 1997 when D1010 Western Campaigner worked an evening Quantock Belle dining train away towards Minehead as the sun highlights the body side detail.